BABY QUOTIENT

Hilariously Real
New Baby Parenting Tips

Written and illustrated by

Grace McKenzie

ISBN: 978-1-7332749-7-5

Copyright © 2019 Nova Meno LLC.
All rights reserved.

#2. Never trust a yellow stain with a newborn in the house.

#4. Carrying playing cards and an iPad for the hospital stay after your baby's delivery is completely useless. There. Is. No. Time.

#5. Make sure you clip your fingernails BEFORE you clean up your baby's poop disaster! (In hindsight, this should be tip #2)

#3. All tips in this book are important irrespective of the sequence you read them in. You've just had a baby. There is no such thing as "order" anymore.

#6. Hospitals are foremost a booming business. Where there is a bill, there is a pay!

#7. You have reached a whole new level of love when you can tolerate spit and pee on you that is not yours and no alcohol is involved.

#8. Babies have very short memory spans... biologically built-in to overcome experiences with rectal thermometers.

#9. Three states of matter can simultaneously coexist inside a freshly soiled diaper.
And on your lucky day... thermonuclear plasma too!

#10. Probability of a puke / pee / poop accident is directly proportionate to the newness of your clothes.

#11. The "sick day / medical leave" policy for parenthood sucks!

#12. The sound of your baby crying is a sure sign that you were comfortable just before hearing it.

#13. That odd hour at night when you are absolutely frustrated that your infant is not sleeping, remember that just like kidney stones and gas, this too shall pass.

#14. Baby Spit-up: An equal opportunity employer since the birth of baby-holding.

#15. You know you need a break when your baby is crying in the background and you start putting your pillow to sleep... while you are still sleeping.

#16. de Quervian's tendonitis of the wrist (a.k.a. Mommy Thumb) due to baby holding. It's a real thing.

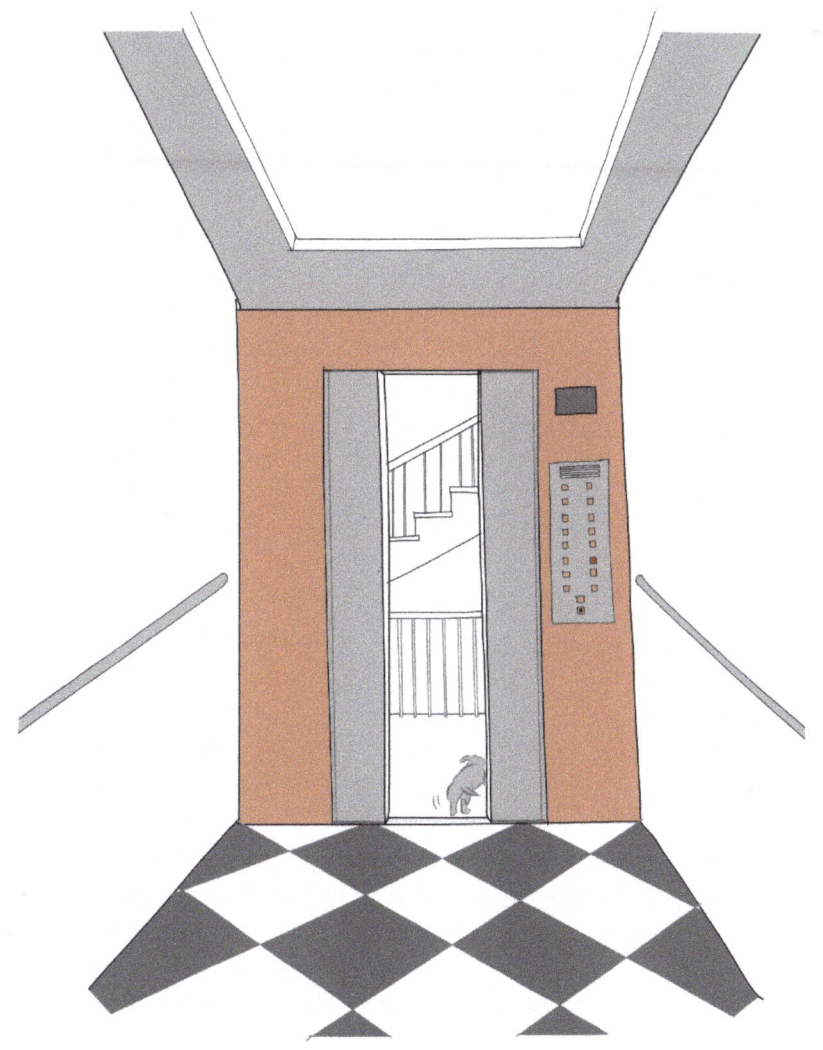

#17. Some people in the elevator can tell the difference between yours and your baby's ~~farts~~ ... umm... burps.

#18. Your baby's sleep is like a unique snowflake! Beautiful, calm, light, impossible to replicate and gone before you know it!

#19. It's strange how pain is funny in retrospect... only once you can sleep more than two hours at a time, of course.

#20. Doodie Call: In a war-like situation when you have to drop everything you are doing to tend to a diaper change.

#21. Drool is like the vodka in a glass of screwdriver. Without the 'OJ Pulp' and in moderation, it is mostly harmless.
PSA - Please drink / spit-up responsibly.

#22. Diapers.
Change is the only constant.

#23. You know your baby is eating well when even the diaper size turns to number 2.

#24. Eventually, you will get your baby's poop on your hands.
... and other places.
... more than once.

#25. If your baby ever cracks the "evil mastermind" club, you would be one of the top two minions. But then... you might already be one.

#26. Mathematics of a new parent's sleep:

6 hours sleep	= 6 hours sleep
3 hours sleep + 1 hour wink + 1.5 hour shut-eye + 1 hour nap	= 3 hours sleep

#27. Within weeks, your baby will have more clothes than you. And within weeks of that, they will be completely useless.

#28. From your baby's perspective... damned if you doodoo, damned if you don't.

#29. As a new parent if you thought you have never been as tired as you are today... just wait for it.

#30. You cannot imagine a real poop-tastrophe until you have seen poop climb up till the armpits!

#31. In all likelihood, adult diapers were invented for parents who had no time getting ready in the morning.
Just maybe.

#32. You can get addicted to that baby smell!

#33. Solid food can truly bring vibrancy to your baby's life... one vividly colored poop at a time.

#34. Your car is the most expensive baby rocker you will ever have.

#35. You can break through the toughest sinus blockages by letting your baby process solid foods. Stink Alert!

#36. The number of poop tips you learn here are directly proportional to reality.

#37. As a new parent if you are wondering when you will finish your work, just remember that almost all superheroes work at night.

#38. When life gives you so much, jammed all together at the same time, things find their own way out. Usually up the back where the diaper opens up.

#39. You realize at some point you have to stop counting your baby's age in weeks.

#40. The soft cartilage of your nose is no match for a head-banging baby.

#41. After having a baby, if you ever thought you had a chance to finish everything you started, then

#42. A PR company's advertisement: If you find yourself celebrating your kid's 49th week or 37th month milestones, you may need professional help.

#43. Forget savoring your gourmet meals. Adhere to an exciting 2-step meal strategy for new parents:
1- Take turns
2- Inhale food

#44. On certain days, that song stuck in your head is a nursery rhyme!

#45. Your infant's mobility is inversely proportional to yours.

#47. Daycare colds are like happiness. They grow the more you share them.

#48. Ever wondered if all the diaper changing is just an investment to get your diapers changed when you are too old?

#49. There comes a day when a question like, "how has my baby not peed / pooped on me yet is eventually answered.

#46. One small step for baby,
one giant headache for baby-proofing!

#50. Daycare.
Your local organic vaccination store.

#51. Over 75% of your sense of taste comes from smell! So the next time you get that really strong whiff from a diaper you know you can practically taste it.

#52. It may take a village to raise a child, but usually about half the village is just Mom!

#1._____

(Tell us about your #1 tip.)

Visit us on:

@BabyQuotient　　@BABYQUOTIENT　　@BabyQuotient

www.ingramcontent.com/pod-product-compliance
Lightning Source LLC
Chambersburg PA
CBHW040045100526
44584CB00033BA/4449